THE COMPLETE BOOK OF

MARDUK

BY NABU

10TH ANNIVERSARY – COLLECTOR'S EDITION

THE COMPLETE BOOK OF

MARDUK

BY NABU

A POCKET ANUNNAKI DEVOTIONAL COMPANION TO BABYLONIAN PRAYERS & RITUALS

Edited & Translated by Joshua Free

PUBLISHED BY THE **JOSHUA FREE** IMPRINT REPRESENTING

Mardukite Truth Seeker Press — mardukite.com

© 2009 – 2019, JOSHUA FREE

ISBN : 978-0-578-47032-0

Being a series of prayers
taught to the priests of Babylon
and the Order of Nabu
as a devotional method for them
to honor the Anunnaki.

Revised Edition—August 2019

LOVINGLY DEDICATED TO:

MARDUK & SARPANIT
*My Lord & Lady of Babylon
—who gave me life.*

&

ANU + ENLIL + ENKI
*The Spirit of the Supernal Trinity
—who gave us all life.*

**MARDUKITE
CHAMBERLAINS**

TABLET OF CONTENTS

MARDUKITE
10TH ANNIVERSARY

PREFACE TO THE 10TH ANNIVERSARY
COLLECTOR'S EDITION

Ten years passed by since materials from the *Book of Marduk by Nabu* started circulating privately among the Mardukite Research Organization (Mardukite Chamberlains), originally connected to a revolutionary discourse known as *Liber-50*, currently available in the 10th Anniversary Collector's Edition "*Gates of the Necronomicon: The Secret Anunnaki Tradition of Babylon*" hardcover anthology, and simultaneously in "*The Sumerian Legacy: A Guide to Esoteric Archaeology.*"

The *Book of Marduk by Nabu* reflects a very real modern philosophical and meta-spiritual "New Thought" movement aligned specifically with the *Anunnaki* paradigm. In ancient Babylon, this was famously founded among the followers of **MARDUK**—recognized among the pantheon as patron of Babylon city and self-made "*King of the Gods*" for this "Mardukite" branch of the Mesopotamian *mythos* with the assistance of the Nabu priesthood of scribes.

Contrary to many other modern Mardukite literary contributions, the Tablet-W series of the *Book of Marduk by Nabu* is not itself based on a transliteration of "ancient" tablets—although inspired by them. In brief: modern self-honest practitioners developed a pocket devotional as a practical supplement to a very real system—where communication with specific "alien intelligences" is sought.

Fundamental work and development conducted by the Mardukite Research Organization from 2008 through 2012 is published as a library of materials known underground as the *Mardukite Core*—or else the *Necronomicon Anunnaki Legacy* (among other names)—is now reaching the global public in its entirety after first existing privately with the Mardukite Chamberlains.

Mardukite Chamberlains made sweeping discoveries and revelations that were all published during the course of their earliest active years. The question, particularly toward *Liber-50*—and materials available throughout the 'Mardukite Core'—is *"how"* this knowledge has been and can be accessed. The only suitable public answer is: *The Book of Marduk by Nabu* (*Liber-W*).

In commemoration of the 10th Anniversary of its release with this beautifully crafted deluxe hardcover collector's edition—I have included supplemental materials first released within the *Book of Marduk by Nabu* series, but only available separate from the original paperback; hence inclusion of the word "complete" in the present title. These include critical excerpts from the *Book of Zagmuk by Nabu* (*Liber-Z*) and the *Book of Gates by Nabu* (*Liber-G*). As an additional bonus, several images have been added for this edition derived from *The Anunnaki Tarot* guidebook recently developed with Kyra Kaos.

Within these pages a newcomer might glean the beauty of the system, but a more adept *seeker* of the mysteries will undoubtedly discover much more with little further suggestions and even less prompting. The resurrection of this *lost book* will most certainly be as well received now as it was <u>ten years</u> ago—if not even more so today, as the work of the *Mardukite Research Organization* continues to reach new and wider global audiences.

May the personal possession of this most treasured tome, bring you infinite blessings as a talisman of Truth!

In Peace, Love & Unity – Always,

~ JOSHUA FREE
Akiti/Akitu – March 2019

INTRODUCTION & APPLICATION
NABU-TUTU SERIES – TABLET IV

We have sealed seven representative stations or gates in BABYLON. While it is true that each of the cities did emphasize their local patrons, a god and a goddess, we have sought a unity for all the gods, under the watchful eye of my father, MARDUK, son of ENKI.

Our father, ENKI, took MARDUK as an apprentice to the magical and religious arts while in E.RIDU and I later took hold of such mysteries and dispersed the knowledge to my scribes and priests in BABYLON and Egypt, where my family was recognized by other names.

The "Seven" are each embodiments of one of the seven Gates forged in BABYLON, homes to the gods of the "younger pantheon." It is true, the same seven-fold division may be found to fragment the *world of form*—corresponding to color, sound, or the planets observed by the ancient ancestors from Earth, seen as *"Guardians."*

The seven planetary systems, which have been connected to the "Seven" of the Gates, also correlate to an easily observable weekly cycle of time. Planet-ruling days offer the supplicant [priest] themes for intention ceremonies or meditation opportunities, each appealing to one of the "sets" of ANUNNAKI "divine couples" honored in the "younger pantheon" of Babylon.

     Sunday – Sun – SHAMMASH [UTU] (& AYA)
     Monday – Moon – NANNA [SIN] (& NINGAL)
     Tuesday – Mars – NERGAl (& ERESHKIGAL)
     Wednesday – Mercury – NABU (& TESHMET)
     Thursday – Jupiter – MARDUK (& SARPANIT)
     Friday – Venus – ISHTAR [INANNA] (& DUMUZI)
     Saturday – Saturn – NINIB [NINURTA] (& BA'U)

Within the combined domains of the "Seven" are all of the material and spiritual aspects a priest or magician seeks in life (e.g. ISHTAR for *love* or SAMAS for *truth*) and one merely must appeal with self-honesty and true words to attain them. This is as the original arts were set down in days of old, left for men to remember us—and we will remember you.

The names and Gates are not merely there for the bedazzlement of the "occult initiate" as you have been taught (there to ascend to and forget about): they are very real "magical skills" and "spiritual lessons" based on the division and the fragmentation of the material universe—a mastery only attainable by a true and faithful relationship with the ANUNNAKI gods of your ancestors.

Man's use of the spiritual power of the gods became subverted, altered and bastardized into the mystical systems now given for your disposal, written by men with no better understanding of the traditions they seek to invoke then those who read them. (And some of these traditions are even falsely said to be derived from my hand.) The true priest or magician compels the gods by friendship and trust, not fear and hatred.

By MARDUK, I learned the power of incantation. I was taught to appease the gods in his name, to speak the words of the higher. MARDUK invoked the name of ENKI, our father, who, invoked the name of ANU. And so was born the magical "hierarchies" that magicians have confused. I taught the magician-scribes of my order to invoke my name and seal during their petitions to the gods, which I have given here, as I learned it from MARDUK. . .

THE GRAND INVOCATION
INCANTATION OF ERIDU

ANU above me, King in Heaven.
ENLIL, Commander of the Airs.
ENKI, Lord of the Deep Earth.
I am NABU – hear my words.
I am the priest of MARDUK and SARPANIT.
Son of our father, ENKI and DAMKINA.
I am the priest in E.RIDU.
I am the magician in BABYLON.
My spell is the spell of ENKI.
My incantation is the incantation of MARDUK.
The Tablets of Destiny, I hold in my hands.
The Ankh of ANU and ANTU, I hold in my hands.
The wisdom of ENLIL and NINLIL, I call to me.
The Magic Circle of ENKI and DAMKINA,
    I conjure about me.
SHAMMASH and AYA are before me.
NANNA-SIN and NINGAL are behind me.
NERGAL and ERESHKIGAL are at my right side.
NINIB-NINURTA and BA'U are at my left side.
The blessed light of ISHTAR and DUMUZI
    shines favorably upon my sacred work.
It is not I, but MARDUK,
    who performs the incantations.

As should become increasingly apparent to contemporary folk of the current age, the ANUNNAKI are powerful and influential, though often directly unseen, forces behind the reality of the life you exist in—as your ancestors were well aware of. If you work with us in conjunction with the natural flow of the universal energies, then you will come face to face with your true destiny—and invited home, again.

Discern your true-knowledge, learn the challenge of self-mastery, and then dear *seeker*, resolve to walk with the gods among the stars, circumnavigating the illusions of this world which have been raised before you as a test of your existence.

> When you have proven yourself before us,
> we shall celebrate your arrival . . .

[Here ends the Nabu-Tutu Tablet IV]

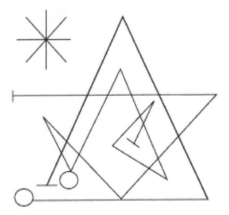

THE BOOK OF

MARDUK

(LIBER-W)

MONDAY

NANNA-SIN

THE MOON

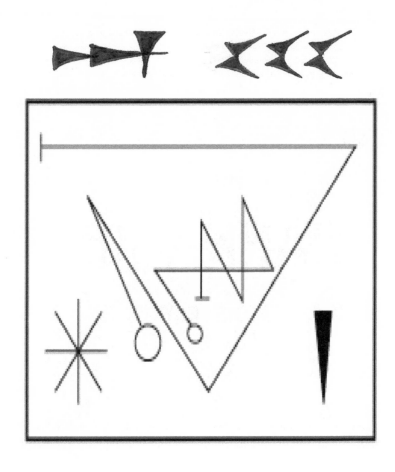

MONDAY — THE MOON — NANNA-SIN

To the ancients, the moon was the "sun at night." It illuminated the path for travelers and kept watch as the people slept. Just as the sun was invoked to grant judgments of the daytime, the moon is given the domain over the dreams of men. Being the first spiritual threshold (Gate) between earth and heaven, the moon is significantly linked to the astral plane. The priestesses (and later witches) of INANNA-ISHTAR revered the moon, called NANNA by Sumerians or Sin to the Babylonians, as their sky-father and/or spiritual-mate. ISHTAR literally was the "daughter of the moon" (and a twin to the sun/SAMAS) and her followers often also took this title.

Our pantheon places NANNA in the position of lunar god with the designation of 30, the basic lunar month of the Sumerian calendar (30 x 12 = 360). The name NANNA (or NANNAR) is actually an attribute of the full moon. He is called *Sin* (or SU.EN) when representing the crescent and the name for the new moon is: *AS.IM.BABBAR.* The lunar current is heavily water oriented with blue hues, though best represented ritually in the non-color spectrum (silver, black, white).

PRAYER TO NANNA & NINGAL

ilu-NANNA. ilu-SIN. ilu-istari-NINGAL.
ilu-NANNAR. ilu-NAMRASIT.
su-bu-u man-za-za ina ilani rabuti
  maru aplu ilu-ENLIL u ilu-NINLIL
nam-rat urru-ka ina sami-i ina sat musi
du natalu, nasaru anabu harranu-dim
u nisu ina bitu sat musi suttu
itti namrasit ina sami-i
kima diparu, kima ilu-SAMAS
samsatu ilu-NANNA namaru suttu
  agu
abu ilu-SAMAS
rimi-nin-ni-ma anaku ____ , apil ____ , sa
  ilu-sa ___ u ilu-istari-su ____ .
ilu-NANNA u ilu-NINGAL rimi-nin-
  ni-ma
kaparu anaku sillatu
  lu-us-tam-mar ilu-ut-ka
petu babu temu
li-iz-ziz ina imni-ya u sumuli-ya
  anaku arad-ka elu
an-un-na-ki ti-i-ru u
  na-an-za-zu

PRAYER TO NANNA & NINGAL

NANNA. SIN. NINGAL.
NANNAR. MOON.
Mighty One among the gods, son of ENLIL
  and NINLIL,
Brightest in the heavens at night,
Keeping watch, protecting weary travelers
And the people in their homes as they sleep.
Your brightness extends through the heavens,
Like a torch – Like a fire-god.
Radiance of NANNA, who reflects the
  dreams of men,
To you was born the SUN.
Be favorable to me, I, __ son of __ , whose
  god is __ and whose goddess is __ .
May NANNA and NINGAL deal graciously
  with me,
Cleanse me of iniquity that I may be free to
  call upon thee.
Open the Gates of your mysteries to me,
Stand on either side of me,
  a servant of the Highest.
May the ANUNNAKI come forth an be
  established.

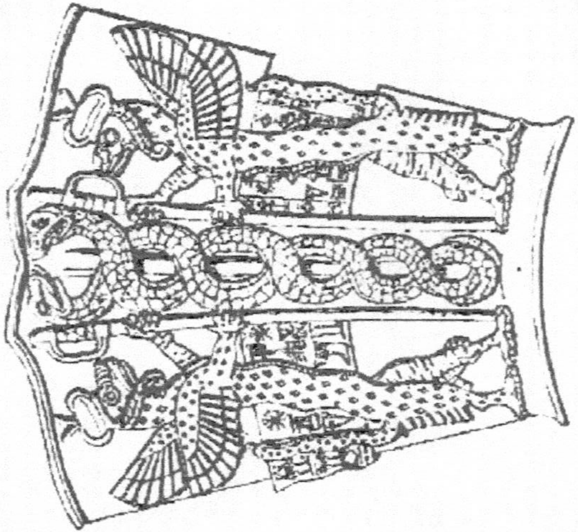

TUESDAY

NERGAL

MARS

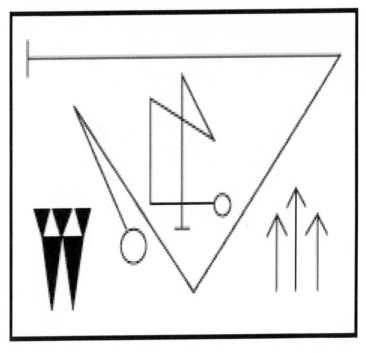

TUESDAY — MARS — NERGAL

The martian current has always been one of the most difficult to properly relay on a spiritual basis. To emphasize the primal fiery destruction would be all too simple. The current is best correlated to the Sumerian concept of "*Girra*" or "*fires of God*." The "hand" of God requires a representative vehicle in which to exercise even its own power in physical ways.

Underlying the power of Mars, and the demonstrator of this force in Babylon (NERGAL), is really "passion." The outer demonstrations of this pure attribute are what can later be deemed by men as lust, love, anger, jealousy and the like. But these are outer forms only – it is the passion, pure and true, that must be embraced. NERGAL is invoked, then, to temper the visions of anger or discord in our lives so we might embrace the passion beneath with clarity, which is anything but evil or destructive. The number of NERGAL is 8, showing that he is outside of the "heavenly" ranks (ending in 5 or 0). His abode is with ERESHKIGAL, who is Queen in the "Underworld." Combined, the pair represent the most "gothic," misunderstood and yet truly romantic elements and attributes of divinity and creation: passion and death.

PRAYER TO NERGAL & ERESHKIGAL

ilu-NERGAL. ilu-IRRIGAL. Ilu-istari-
  ERESHKIGAL. ilu-ERRA.
siru belu ersetu
ilu-istari-ERESHKIGAL, beltu ersetu
saqu-su manzazu
  it-ti ilani samu
ilu-NERGAL u ilu-istari-ERESHKIGAL
rimi-nin-ni-ma, ana-ku ___ , apil ____ ,
  sa ilu-su ___ ilu-istar-su ___ .
banu-ya libbu alalu
di-ni uzzu ina ramanu libbu
ana-ku izuzzu mahru ze
petu babu temu
rimi-nin-ni-ma ina damu
  u du lemnutu seg ina ramanu zi
ana-ku arad-ka elu kamazu ze
  rimi-nin-ni-ma
babu-mah du pataru
an-un-na-ki ti-i-ru u
  na-an-za-zu

PRAYER TO NERGAL & ERESHKIGAL

NERGAL. IRRIGAL. ERESHKIGAL.
ERRA. MARS.
Exalted Lord of the Underworld.
ERESHKIGAL, Queen of the Underworld.
Great is your place
  among the gods of heaven.
NERGAL and ERESHKIGAL,
Truly have mercy on me, __ , son of ___ ,
  whose god is ___ , whose goddess is ___ .
May your hearts be tempered.
Temper also the anger within my heart,
That I may stand before you,
Make me perfect to call upon you,
Open the Gates of your understanding to me.
Grant me a favorable death
  and keep evil from me in life.
I, a servant of the Highest, kneel before thee,
  take pity on me.
May the Great Doors stand open.
May the ANUNNAKI return and
  be established.

WEDNESDAY

NABU

MERCURY

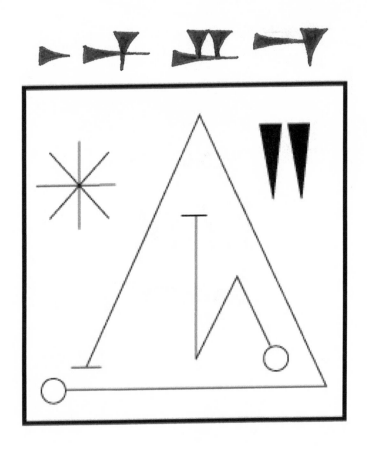

WEDNESDAY — MERCURY — NABU

The *Mercurial* current is connected to divination: relaying information through the universe, or else, communication. Whether it is prayers, a song, the recording of history or the prediction of the future, the performance is undertaken by the blessing of the "scribe-messenger" of the gods. "*Thoth*" or "*Hermes*" is sometimes identified for this current, demonstrating the connection to magic systems, occultism and the air element. Babylonian tradition observes me, NABU, as son of MARDUK, as the scribe-priest of the gods, the keeper of the "destinies" among the younger pantheon with the designation of 12 (connecting heavenly-time and earth-time).

My scribe-priests worked diligently during the Babylonian era forging tablet texts based on the Sumerian tradition, supporting our local patron, MARDUK, as *King of the Gods*, usurping the position of ENLIL and usurping the rights of the position by NINURTA for both spiritual and physical politics. This travesty in Babylon that we conducted, but which is being currently resolved, shows the power of knowledge, true or false, and how it can be used to shape people and the world. Invoke my name for clarity and discernment in the seeking of truth. My color is blue.

PRAYER TO NABU & TESHMET

ilu-NABU. ilu-TUTU. ilu-istari-TESHMET
  ilu-istari-TASMIT. ilu-NEBOS.
tupsarru si-mat ilani
sarru nam-zu si-mat ilani
asaridu bukur ilu-MARDUK u ilu-
  SARPANIT
ilu-NABU na-as duppu si-mat
  ilani
ramanu ur-hi suttu
  lid-mi-ik
ilu-NABU u ilu-TASMITU
  ka-ba-a si-ma-a suk-na ya-si-sa
rimi-nin-ni-ma, ana-ku ___ , apil ___ sa
  ilu-sa ___ u ilu-istari-su ___ .
ebbu ramanu nam-eme-sig u ummuqu
  si-mi-i su-pi-ya
petu babu temu
amat a-kab-bu-u kima a-kab-bu-u
  lu-u ma-ag-rat
sumu-ka ka-lis ina pi nisi ta-a-ab
anaku arad-ka elu
an-un-na-ki ti-i-ru u
  na-an-za-zu

PRAYER TO NABU & TESHMET

NABU. TUTU. TESHMET – TASMIT(U).
NEBOS. MERCURIOS.
Scribe among the Gods,
Keeper of the Wisdom of the Gods,
Firstborn of MARDUK and SARPANIT.
NABU, Bearer of the Tablet of Destinies
  of the gods,
May my dreams [destiny] be filled with
  prosperity.
May my petitions fall on the ears of
  NABU & TASMIT.
Be favorable to me, I, __ son of __ , whose
  god is __ and whose goddess is __ .
Cleanse me of false knowledge, that I might
  be ft to call upon thee.
Open the Gates of your understanding to me.
Bless my mouth with true words to speak
  the prayers.
May the prayers rise from the lips of the
  people.
I am a servant of the Highest,
May the ANUNNAKI come forth and be
  established.

THURSDAY

MARDUK

JUPITER

THURSDAY — JUPITER — MARDUK

The industrious and raw expansive power of Jupiter is placed at the height of most 'Olympian' pantheons (*Zeus* or similar). "Jupiter" comes from the Romans: *Dys Pater*, meaning "Father-God." This energy current commands outright worldly success and the magic of spirits: command of the "Celestial" hierarchies. Elder Gods originally attributed this position to ENLIL in Sumer. I personally heralded my father, MARDUK, into Enlilship of the "younger pantheon" in Babylon. Our tradition there, and in Egypt, was wholly based on him being the centralized figure. Invoke my father for his strength and power, as well as a petitioner to the Elder Gods.

He is exalted as the Master of Magicians, carrying the mysteries of my grandfather, ENKI, to Babylon, and bestowing the traditions upon me to relay. The original designation of Jupiter is 50, the number attributed first to ENLIL and later to MARDUK by the Babylonians, who first was given the number 10. The color of the current is purple, but also airy and fiery colors (yellow, orange, black). This energy is preferred by many leaders and law enforcing folk, lending to those who are pure to receive it, the power to command the material world.

PRAYER TO MARDUK & SARPANIT

ilu-MAR.DUG. ilu-MAR.DUK. ilu-istari-
   ZARPANIT. ilu-silik-MULU.KHI DIL.GAN.
lugal arali, belu asipu
ilu-su BAB.ILI
ilu-SARPANIT(UM), belitu istari-su BAB.ILI
gasru u sapsu ina an-ki
   zi atwu
belu u belitu su BAB.ILI
maharu ramanu arua abnu-gesnu, abnu-
   uqnu u hurasu
dinu-ma ramanu lid-mi-ik
anaku ___ apil ___ sa ilu-su ___ u
   ilu-istar-su ___ .
lu-us-tam-mar ilu-ut-ka
   u atwu ramanu maharu karabu
petu babu temu – petu babu idu
ina ki-bi-ti-ka sir-ti lu-ub-lut lu-us-lim-ma
napsiti narbu ramanu ki-bi su
   su-sud ilani samu
anaku arad-ka elu
an-un-na-ki ti-i-ru u
   na-an-za-zu

PRAYER TO MARDUK & SARPANIT

MARDUK. MERODACH. SARPANIT.
MULU-KHI. JUPITER.
Lord of the Lands, Master of Magicians,
God of Babylon.
SARPANIT, Lady of Babylon.
Mighty and powerful on earth and heaven
  are your words.
Lord and Lady of Babylon,
Accept my offerings of alabaster, lapis lazuli
  and gold.
Judge my life favorably,
I ___ , son of ____ , whose god is ____ , and
  whose goddess is ____ .
Make me fit to behold your divinity
  and teach me to receive thy blessings.
Open the Gates of your power to me.
Let me live. Let me be perfect.
Command greatness in my life as your
  expansion permeates the gods of heaven.
I am a servant of the Highest.
May the ANUNNAKI come forth and
  be established.

FRIDAY

ISHTAR

VENUS

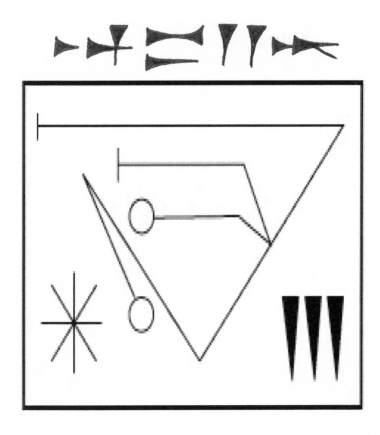

FRIDAY — VENUS — ISHTAR

Most famous among energetic currents of these mysteries is Venusian. It is always dedicated to the "goddess of love and war." A determined goddess, she made her place among all ancient pantheons: whether *Isis, Aphrodite, Ashtoreth*... she is also known as the "goddess of witches," and celebrated in their rites. In Babylon, by request of MARDUK, her political anger was appeased by being established as ISHTAR (Venus).

When ISHTAR and MARDUK were not pair-bonded (as intended), each took it upon themselves to elevate and usurp their own positions among our "younger pantheon."

The Venusian current (and that of Jupiter) are extremely powerful and actively raw energies. They are not always as obvious with their executions, such as you might find with the Sun or Mars, but they store mass amounts of energy for eventual release at the most "propitious" or favorable times. ISHTAR may be invoked to channel energies directed toward the acquisition of desires. (A wise one will be certain this is for their higher good first.) Her number is 15. Colors are green, yellow-green and white, and her elements are water and earth.

PRAYER TO ISHTAR & DUMUZI

ilu-INANNA. ilu-istari-ISHTAR. ilu-
DUMUZI. ilu-ISTAR.
belitu, martu-su ilu-NANNA-SIN
  sa karabu ina samu
ramu-su ilu-ANU, rabianu samu
namru-sat musi
lu-dub-gar-ra sat musi
li-iz-ziz ilu-istari-ya ina sumili-ya
  sutlumu karabu nissanu sabu u ilani
ilu-istari-ISHTAR u ilu-DUMUZI
rimi-nin-ni-ma, ana-ku ___ apil ___ sa
  ilu-sa ___ u ilu-istar-su ___
mesu-ya nigussu, anaku aga
  simtu maharu zi qistu
petu babu temu
li-iz-ziz ramanu manahtu-su zid
a-mat a-kab-bu-u kima a-kab-bu-u lu-u
  ma-ag-rat
is-ti-' nam-ri-ir-ri-ki lim-mi-ru samu
  kima nasaru sabu-su karabu
si-lim itti ya-a-tu-u anaku arad-ka elu
an-un-na-ki ti-i-ru u
  na-an-za-zu

PRAYER TO ISHTAR & DUMUZI

INANNA. ISHTAR. DUMUZI.
ISTARI VENUS.
Queen, Daughter of the Moon,
* who is blessed by the heavens,*
Beloved of ANU, Command in Heaven,
Brightness of the Evening,
Huntress of the Night,
Do come to stand favorably at my side,
* grant me the fruits of men and gods.*
ISHTAR and DUMUZI,
Be favorable to me, I, ___ son of ___ , whose
* god is ___ and whose goddess is ___ ,*
Cleanse me of impurity make me a vessel
* fit to receive your rewards.*
Open the Gates of your understanding to me.
May my actions be true.
May the words I speak bring me to success.
May your light shinning in the heavens
* be a guide to all men you bless favorably.*
Bless me, a servant of the Highest.
May the ANUNNAKI come forth and
* be established.*

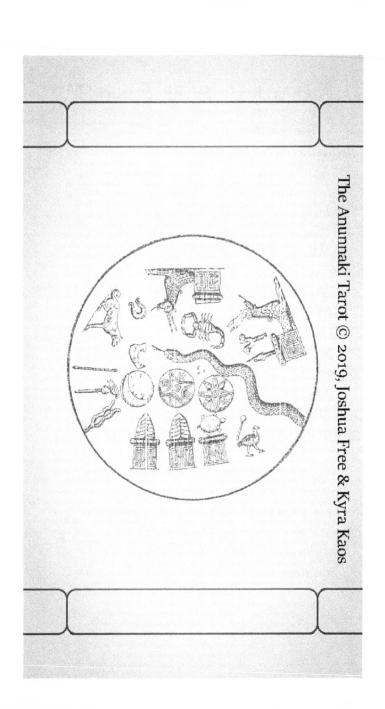

SATURDAY

NINURTA

SATURN

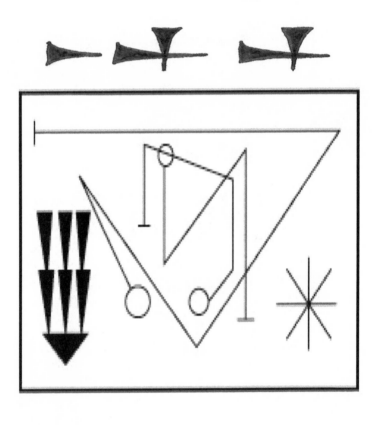

SATURDAY — SATURN — NINURTA

Among planets, Saturn is traditionally dark and secretive, representing hidden power and the "*hidden key*" by which one may be released from the material world of Gates and illusions.

The Saturnalian current is a threshold to the Outer Ones that the secret societies and mystery schools have covertly sought through the ages. NINURTA represents Saturn in Mesopotamia. He also reflects the dark secret of Babylon: He is the heir to *Enlilship*, a position assumed by MARDUK.

In the Babylonian system, NINURTA is given a designation of 4. This indicates he is outside of the 'Olympian pantheon' of 'sky gods,' waiting to take his place, being heir of ENLIL with the number 50. Saturn energy is just as passively introspective as it is actively reflecting the outer world. These lessons demand confronting dark, repressed, guilt-laden aspects of themselves to ascend to self-honest wholeness. The elements of *air* and *earth* are both present in this current and the darker color spectrum is most resonant. Invoke NINURTA to aid in one's own path toward mastery in addition to giving recognition to correct the aspects that have kept the very system from achieving its own wholeness.

PRAYER TO NINURTA & BA'U

ilu-NINURTA. ilu-NINIB. ilu-istari-BA'U.
  ilu-ADAR.
siptu aplu gas-ru bukur ilu-ENLIL
su-bu-u man-za-za ina ilani rabuti
  siru rubu-su ilu-ENLIL u ilu-NINMAH
belu u beltu sihip same u erseti
ilu-NINIB u ilu-istari-BA'U
atwu karabu-ya kisalmahu
ana-ku ___ apil ___ sa ilu-su ___ u
  ilu-istar-su ___
an-ni pu-tur
sir-ti pu-sur
lu-us-tam-mar ilu-ut-ka
  u atwu ramanu lid-mi-ik
petu babu temu,
  anaku arad-ka elu
ilu-istar-BA'U, biltu sur-bu-tu, sela ummu
ilu-NINIB, nisirtu qarradu ilu-ENLIL
ki-bit narbu ramanu zi
si-lim itti ya-a-tu-u
sumu-ka ka-lis ina pi nisi ta-a-ab
an-un-na-ki ti-i-ru u
  na-an-za-zu

PRAYER TO NINURTA & BA'U

NINURTA. NINIB. BA'U.
ADAR. SATURN.
Mighty firstborn son of ENLIL.
Great is your place among the gods,
* royal prince of ENLIL and NINMAH.*
Lord and Lady of the heavenly abode,
NINIB and BA'U,
Speak favorably of me in your courts,
I, ___ , son of ___ , whose god is ____ , and
* whose goddess is ____ .*
Absolve me of my sins.
Remove my iniquities.
Make me fit to call upon and receive your
* blessings.*
Open the Gates of you Understanding to me,
* a servant of the Highest,*
BA'U, Mighty Lady, merciful mother.
NINIB, hidden warrior of ENLIL.
Command greatness in my life.
Look upon me favorably.
May your name be in the mouth of the people.
May the ANUNNAKI return and
* be established.*

SUNDAY

SHAMMASH

THE SUN

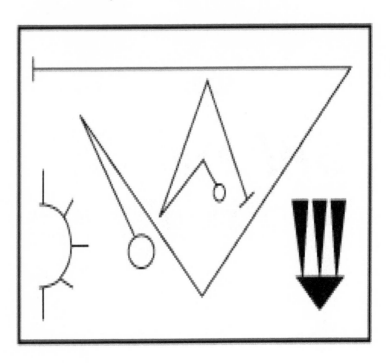

SUNDAY — THE SUN — SHAMMASH

The sun represents the brilliance and radiance of life on earth. It is the light that allows organic life to grow and it is also the manner in which time is divided, including a lifespan. The sun also symbolizes expansive powerful energy and is often invoked for general success and well-being in this existence (and the next). The fiery nature of the star is called to "incinerate iniquities" and also to reveal darkness or lies: the revelation of truth. Mistaken as monotheistic solar worship, the veneration of the sun is the celebration of life, and so annual festivals were marked by the path of the sun (at solstices and equinoxes).

As a representative of "Heaven," the sun signifies the physical presence and watchful eye of "God" invoked to bring righteous judgment to critical situations.

In the Babylonian pantheon, the solar designation of 20 is given to SAMAS (*Shammash*) also known by the Sumerians as UTU. The colors of this energy current are bright (yellow, white, gold) and the dominant element is clearly fire or *starfire*. The prayer that follows, invokes SAMAS to come forth and be established as the supreme judge of the destinies of men on earth.

PRAYER TO SHAMMASH & AYA

ilu-SHAMMASH. ilu-UTU. ilu-istari-AYA.
ilu-SAMAS. samsu.
anqullu u igigallu
dinu ilani
maru aplu ilu-NANNA-SIN
sapiru nam-simtu apitu
ilu-SAMAS u ilu-AYA
karabu danu simtu
metequ damaqu
la-kasadu immu kararu
ilu-SAMAS u ilu-AYA
si-lim itti ya-a-tu-u ___ , apil ___ ,
* sa ilu-sa ___ , ilu-istar-su ___ .*
napahu ramanu sir-tu
lu-ub-lut lu-us-lim-ma maharu nuru
enu atwu uznu ilu-ENLIL
petu babu temu
sumu-ka ka-lis ina pi nisi ta-a-ab
qibitu nig-silim ina ramanu
* napistu*
ana-ku arad-ka elu
an-un-na-ki ti-i-ru u
* na-an-za-zu.*

PRAYER TO SHAMMASH & AYA

SHAMMASH. UTU. AYA.
SAMAS. SUN.
Fiery and Powerful One,
Judge among the gods,
Son of the Moon-god,
Overseer of the destinies of the lands.
SHAMMASH and AYA,
Be the favorable judges of my destiny.
May the path be prosperous.
Unequaled light of day,
SHAMMASH and AYA
Shine favorably on me, __ , son of __ ,
  whose god is __ and whose goddess is __ .
Incinerate my iniquities.
Make me perfect to behold your light.
Lord, who appeals to the ears of ENLIL,
Open the Gates of your understanding to me.
Permanent is your mighty word on earth.
May your unquestioned command dictate
  prosperity in my life.
I am a servant of the Highest,
May the ANUNNAKI return and
  be established.

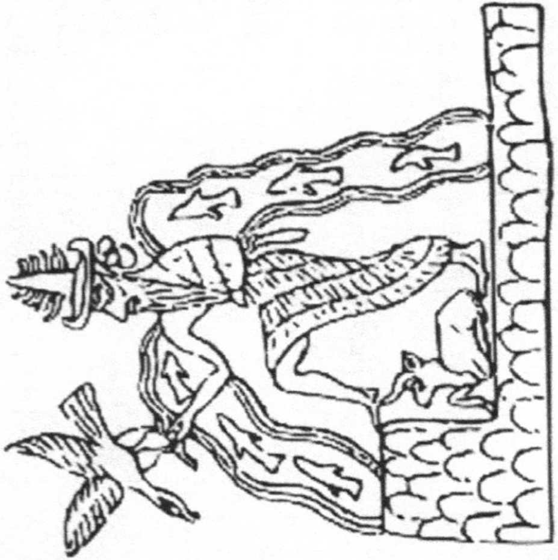

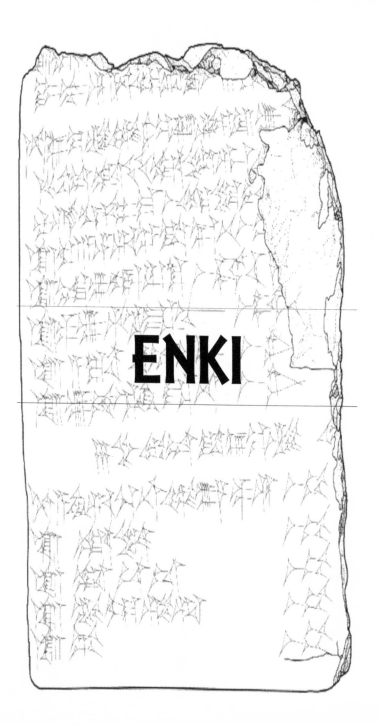

ENKI

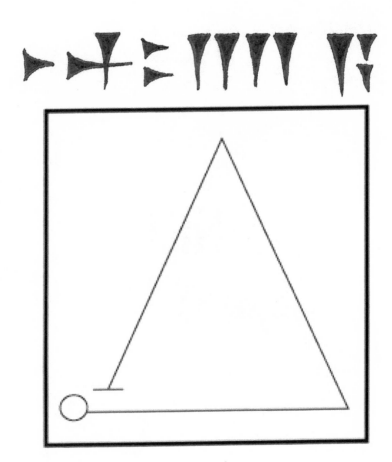

SUPERNAL – E.A.–ENKI – NEPTUNE

ENKI assisted his brother ENLIL in developing the local universe, pre-Babylonian Sumer, and the organization of the physical world. Later, ENKI or E.A. ("Whose House is Water") is given domain over physical manifestation and creation in the form of "magic." In Babylon we gave to him the name of EN.KI meaning "Lord of the Earth." In raising him to this position among the people it was much easier for his son, MARDUK, to be given a high station as well.

The elements *earth* and *air* are strong in this energetic current. ENKI is sometimes referred to as "Our Father" among *our* Race of Marduk. He is given charge of the *"Word of Power"* [called MAAT by the Egyptians] that charges the incantations of magic that breathe changes into the universe. These secrets were passed onto MARDUK and myself. They became the foundation of our traditions in Babylon and Egypt. As a planetary power, ENKI is Neptune, the Greek "Poseidon of the Deep." His power is ancient and strong knowing no boundaries in the universe. For a time he had in his possession the Anunnaki *Tablet of Destiny* – the 'Arts of Civilization' powering the magic of the priests in Babylon.

PRAYER TO ENKI & DAMKINA

ilu-E.A ilu-IA ilu-EN.KI
ilu-istari-NIN.KI ilu-istari-DAM.KI.NA
ilu-EN.KI samu-ya sa mesari eresti
ilu-istari-DAM.KI.NA sar-rat kal
  an-un-na-ki ilani la-tu
ilu-EN.KI u ilu-istari-DAM.KI.NA
  sur-ba-ti ina ilani
  la-u parsuki
rimi-nin-ni-ma anaku ___ apil ___ sa
  ilu-sa ___ u ilu-istari-sa ___
abu u ummu kispu
nabatu kabasu ramanu manahtu
rasanu-ya rigmu ina ramanu siptu
ki-bi-ma lis-si-mi zik-ri
amat a-kab-bu-u kima a-kab-bu-u
  lu-u ma-ag-rat
dinu-ma ramanu lid-mi-ik
lu-us-tam-mar ilu-ut-ka nabatu anaku
  arad-ka elu
an-un-na-ki ti-i-ru u
  na-an-za-zu
u emedu salimu menu u tes
  enu zid katamu [AN.KI] sihip
  same u eresti

PRAYER TO ENKI & DAMKINA

EA. IA. ENKI.
NINKI. DAMKINA.
ENKI, Your name is the depths of the Earth.
DAMKINA, Queen among the Anunnaki
  Gods
ENKI and DAMKINA,
  You are great among the gods,
  Mighty is your command.
Be favorable to me ___ son of ___ whose
  god is ___ and whose goddess is ___ .
Father and Mother of Magic,
Shine upon my work.
Be the voice of my incantations.
Speak and let the Word by heard.
Let the Word I speak, when I speak it,
  be favorable.
Open the Gates of your understanding.
Judge my existence favorably.
Let your Divine Light shine through me,
  a servant of the Highest.
May the Anunnaki come forth and
  be established.
And may peace, love and unity,
  reign true throughout the Universe.

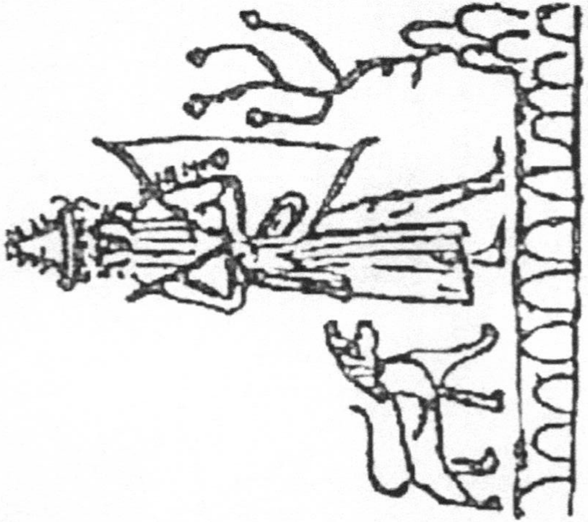

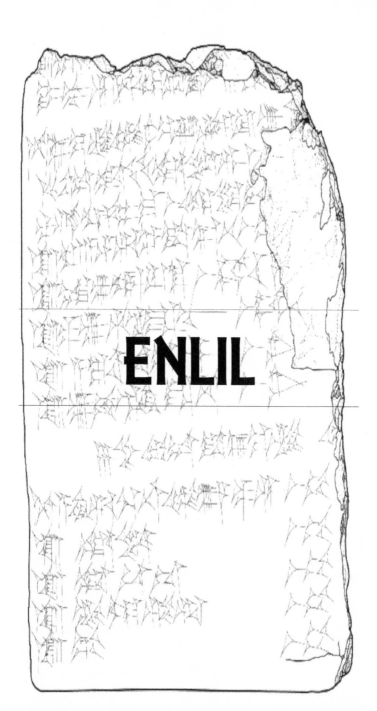

ENLIL

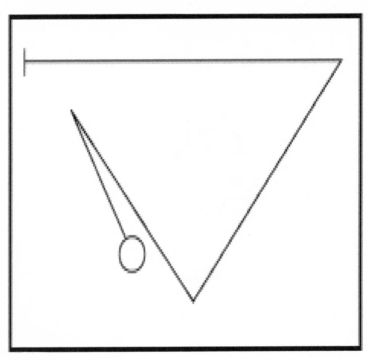

SUPERNAL – ENLIL (EL) – ELDER-JUPITER

ENLIL is "Lord of the Command" – heir to *Anuship* in 'Heaven', position of 'God' in the local universe. This shift in power began the Judeo-Semitic age, when ENLIL appeared to the people of the "Holy Lands" as "Jehovah." It can be said that EN-LIL is indeed the "God" of the Israelites and the Judeo-Christian and Islamic traditions.

Duality split the pantheon between lineages of ENLIL and ENKI occurred on Earth and in Heaven. ENLIL should be rightfully acknowledged as the power of *Anuship* in modern times, with his own heir, NINURTA as successor. Such was the original arrangement for the last age and for the "peace, love and unity to reign true in the Universe," it is essential that the perceptions of these traditions, in addition to their realizations in modern times, is carried in self-honesty.

Jupiter is the original current of ENLIL, though we observe MARDUK in Babylon, and the power to execute "*Anuship*" in the material world – an exercise of power in elemental domains of *air* and *fire* elements. Where ENKI is "Lord of the Earth," ENLIL is seen as "Lord of the Airs," the intermediary space bonding (between) the earth and the heavens.

PRAYER TO ENLIL & NINLIL

ilu-ENLIL ilu-BEL
ilu-istari-NINLIL ilu-istari-BELTU
sumu-ya sa dug-ga
rigmu-ya dug-ga samu u erseti
ilu-ENLIL abu ilani
ilu-BEL-ENLIL u ilu-istari-
  BELITU-NINLIL
zi kima ramanu abu u ummu anaku ___
  apil ___ sa ilu-su ___
  ilu-istari-su ___
ka-ba-a sutlumu ramanu tehu
  u amaru dingir-ya itti ilani
sutlumu-lu manzazu-ya itti ilani masu
banu anaku aga zaku temu
petu babu temu
karabu ramanu manahtu
  u zaqtu napharu
lu-us-tam-mar ilu-ut-ka nabatu anaku
  arad-ka elu
qibitu narbu ina [An.Ki] sihip same u eresti
an-un-na-ki ti-i-ru u
  na-an-za-zu
u emedu salimu menu u tes
  enu zid katamu [An.Ki] sihip same u eresti

PRAYER TO ENLIL & NINLIL

ENLIL. BEL.
NINLIL. BELTU.
Your name is the command.
Your voice rules the Heavens and Earth.
ENLIL, Father of the Gods,
BEL-ENLIL and BELITU-NINLIL,
You are as a father and mother to me ___ ,
  son of ___ , whose god is ____ and whose
  goddess is ____ .
At your command, allow me to approach
  and behold your divinity among the gods.
Let not your place among the gods
  be forgotten.
Make me a vessel of clear understanding.
Open the Gates of your understanding to me.
Bless me in my workings
  and show me wholeness.
Let your divine light shine through me,
  a servant of the Highest.
Command greatness in the Universe.
May the Anunnaki come forth and
  be established,
 And may peace, love and unity
   reign true throughout the Universe.

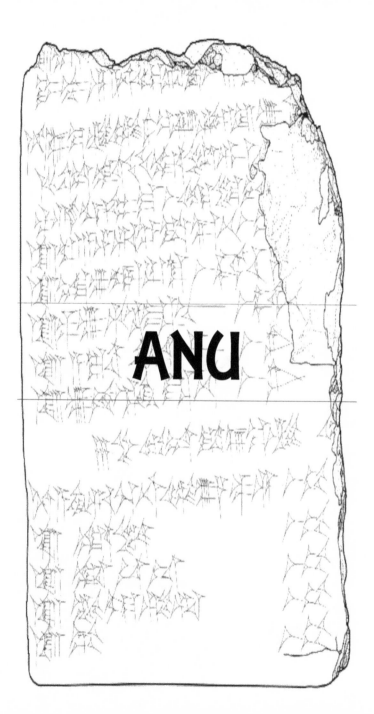

ANU

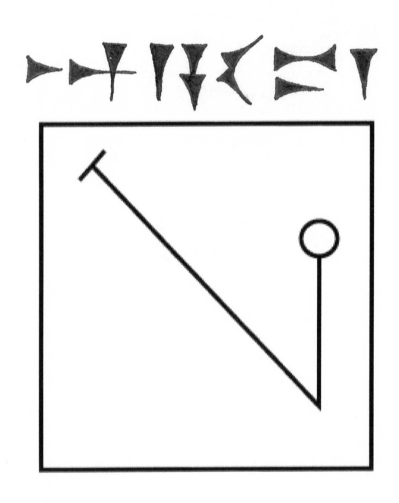

SUPERNAL – ANU (AN) – URANUS

From the start of recorded history in Sumer, cuneiform tablets kept by NABU *priest-scribes* , it is ANU who is given role of "Father in Heaven," All-Father of the gods. This is what He was to us all, the father of both ENLIL and ENKI. All members of the Anunnaki pantheon from both lineages are His children.

The *"House of Anu"* is the "domain of Heaven," also the name given to the planet Uranus [UR-ANU]. His heavenly force has not always been immediately felt on earth, and has instead, been left to his heirs, ENLIL and ENKI, to command the cosmos in his stead.

ANU, the blessed Father of us all, shall ever remain in the mouth of the people – in the prayers. His legacy shall always remain on epic tablets and through the deeds of his children. His place in Heaven shall always be known to us, though it will be filled by another, as ANU has left us now with only his Shade remaining – and a position in the heavens meant to be filled by ENLIL (and his successor, NINURTA). With the dawning of the New Age comes another change in divinity. Let self-honest peace, love and unity reign true through the Universe when it does.

PRAYER TO ANU & ANTU

ilu-ANU ilu-AN ilu-AN.NA
  ilu-istari-AN.TU
ilu-ANU abu ina samu
ilu-AN.NA samu-sa zi nigul sumu
daru-sa zi gitmalu-ya amatu
duru-sa zi dingir-ya edullu
zi biritu [an.sar] samu u [ki.sar] erseti
  sa-zi u'uru
madu ilani
  duru risatu zi mulammu
guhsu-ya gistaggu
  la urru
ilu-istaru-AN.TU ummu samu u nabalu
si-lim itti-ya a-tu-u
dingir hamdan ina samu lu-us-tam-mar
  itu-ut-ka u atwu ramanu lid-mi-ik
anaku ___ apil ___ sa ilu-su ___
  ilu-istar-su ___
anaku izuzzu wasru gudmu zi
anaku arad-ka-ya
  arad-ka elu
an-un-na-ki ahurru-ya
  ti-i-ru u na-an-za-zu

PRAYER TO ANU & ANTU

ANU. AN. ANNA.
  Goddess, ANTU.
ANU, Father in Heaven.
Heaven is your everlasting name.
Eternal is your perfect Word.
Forever is your Divine Kingdom.
The domain of Heaven and Earth
  is yours to command.
May the Great Gods
  ever rejoice in your splendor.
May your Altar of Offering
  never be empty.
ANTU, Mother of the Sky and Land,
Be favorable to me.
Divine Union of Heaven, make me fit
  to call upon and receive your blessings.
I, son of ___ whose god is ___ and whose
  goddess is ___ ,
Stand humbly before thee in praise.
I am thy servant –
  a servant of the Highest.
May the Anunnaki, your children,
  come forth and be established.

*Being a series of rituals
taught to the priests of Babylon
and the Order of Nabu
as a devotional method for citizens
to celebrate the New Year
and the Supremacy of Marduk.*

THE BOOK OF

ZAGMUK

(LIBER Z)

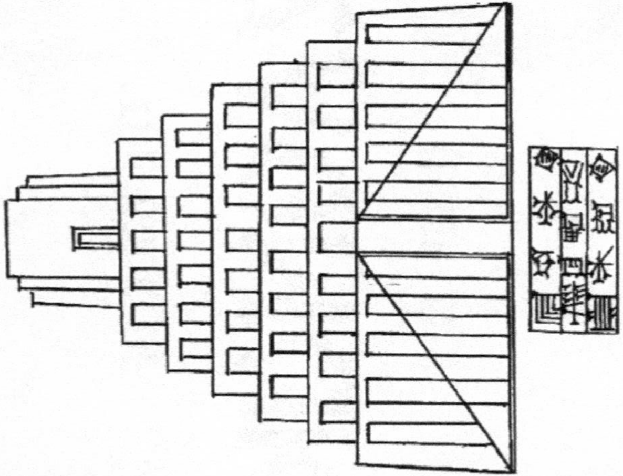

INTRODUCTION & APPLICATION
A.KI.TI / A.KI.TU FESTIVAL RITE

In ancient *Babylon*, the New Year Festival was the central most religio-political "Mardukite" event marking the beginning of the annual cycle. At that time in "celestial history," the spring equinox observation of *Akitu* (or *Akiti*) coincided with the sun entering the "*Aries*" zone, the zodiacal sign of MARDUK. This spring festival symbolized not only agricultural fertility and renewal of the land on earth, but also a restatement or reinforcement of the national position of MARDUK and his role in the universe.

The Akkadian name for the final day of the festival—*Akiti* or *Akitu*—translates roughly to "*On Earth, Life.*" Most scholars usually only recognize the "agricultural" significance and not necessarily the "political" and "mystical" functions of the observation. True, the *Akitu* festival took place twelve days before the annual crops were planted—but, this large public national "celebration" also reconfirmed supremacy of MARDUK and his position in the *Babylonian* Anunnaki Pantheon, making it the single most important ancient "holiday" for the Mardukite tradition.

After a time of gods had come and gone, the priests and kings continued to observe these ceremonial customs using representative "images" or statuary to symbolized the "divine presence" of MARDUK and NABU as they made a procession each year through the streets of *Babylon*. Each of the twelve festival days begins at dawn. The High Priest of the "Temple of Marduk"—the E.SAG-ILA or "House of Marduk"—goes and prepares the temple and other ceremonial areas before dawn, then makes a "general invocation" to MARDUK, before the "image" (statue) of the god in his shrine.

INVOCATION PRAYER TO MARDUK

MARDUK, Almighty, Powerful One of ASURA,
Exalted, Noble-Blood, Firstborn of ENKI,
Almighty MARDUK,
Who causes the ITURA to rejoice, Lord of the ESAGILA,
Aid to BABYLON, Lover of the EZIDA, Preserver of Life,
Prince of IMAHTILLA, Renewer of Life,
Shadow over the Land,
Protector of Foreign Lands,
Forever is MARDUK the Sovereign of Shrines,
Forever is MARDUK the Name in the mouth of
   the people.
Almighty Lord MARDUK,
At your command the Earthborn remain alive,
At your command let me live, let me be perfect,
Let me behold your divinity.
What I will to be, let me obtain my wishes.
MARDUK, cause righteousness to come from
   my mouth,
MARDUK, cause mercy to dwell in my heart,
Return to the Earth; re-establish the ANUNNAKI
   and command mercy.
May my God stand at my right hand.
May my Goddess stand at my left hand.
May my Lord who is favorable to the stars, stand
   firmly at my side,
To speak the Word of Command, to hear my prayer
   and show favor,
When I speak, let the words be powerful.
Almighty Lord MARDUK, come and command life.
BEL's Fires go with you, ENKI smile upon us all.
May the Elder Gods delight in your mercy.
May the Earth Deities be favorable to thee and me.

THE FIRST DAY

On the first day of the festival, *after* the priests carried out morning services, the King accompanies a procession around the city of *Babylon*, showing the people that he carried the official "royal" regalia of his position—the "*Crown of Anu*," the *Scepter of Dragonblood*, &tc. This is to secure the symbolism of "worldly material reign" firmly in the consciousness of the population. Transfer of this power to the king by the gods demonstrates his "*Divine Right to Rule.*" Then, portions of the "*Enuma Eliš*" (Mardukite Tablet-N) are read to prove that Marduk is authorized to dispense this "divine right."

THE SECOND DAY

During the second day, the *High Priest* is charged to ritually cleanse the temple with consecrated waters from both rivers of *Babylon*—the *Tigris* and the *Euphrates.* Sweet fragrances of juniper and cypress fill the air. The official image (statue) of NABU is carried from the nearby city of *Borsippa* and left just outside of *Babylon* at the *Uras Gate.* The sacred symbols of "worldly material reign" are removed from the King by the *High Priest* and taken by procession to the *Temple of Marduk*, where the symbols are placed before the (statue) feet of the *god.* These "sacred objects" are only "returned" to MARDUK briefly, so that the *Anunnaki King* may dispense them "officially" back to the *Earthly King* who rules the Babylonian nation in the name of MARDUK. This also demonstrates to all concerned that these symbols of reign are only "borrowed" by kings, who are really "stewards" for MARDUK on Earth. The statue of MARDUK is brought outside the *Esagila* and the King makes his appeal to rule before it. Then, the items of power are returned to the King by the *High Priest*, and a procession ensues back to the palace, showing the people that the King has been granted the "Divine Right" by MARDUK.

THE THIRD DAY

Day three involves a reenactment of the "*Enuma Eliš*," followed by a procession of the image/statue of NABU on a pathway of reeds. NABU is brought before the Sumerian "*Temple of Ninurta*" (sometimes called the "*Temple of Fifty*") where he is to "defeat" two enemies ("*evil gods*") in the name of MARDUK. A dramatization is performed—two statues are destroyed before his image. NABU is then left at the "*Temple of Ninurta*" until the sixth day of the festival.

THE FOURTH, FIFTH & SIXTH DAY

On the fourth day, both statues are ritually "cleansed" by the *High Priest*. The image of MARDUK is returned to the *Esagila*, where MARDUK is symbolically "imprisoned within the mountain" (or the "pyramid")—which had happened during the fall of the first "Tower of Babel" in prehistory. In one account, he is trapped is by "two evil gods," presumably the same ones that NABU defeats. A more accurate explanation according to tradition is that his imprisonment was political punishment for the death of *Dumuzi* (or *Tammuz*)—consort of INANNA-ISHTAR. MARDUK remains "buried alive"—*dead but dreaming*—for three days. During this, on the fifth day, the epic cycle of INANNA-ISHTAR—known as (Mardukite Tablet-C or) the "*Descent to the Underworld*"—is recited (or dramatized) and NABU finally enters the city again on the sixth day.

THE SEVENTH AND EIGHTH DAY

Ceremonial applications of the seventh day are derived from a wisdom series, given as Mardukite Tablets I, II and III of the *Nabu-Tutu (Tablet-T)* series. Here, the young prophet-son deity—NABU—approaches the *voice* of the "*unseen god*," MARDUK as *Amon-Ra* entrapped in the "pyramid." During the festival, NABU—the statue/image of

THE GREAT HYMN TO MARDUK

*Among the multitudes of men who exist and
  have names,*
*Who is there that can of himself have True-
  Knowledge?*
*Who has not erred on Earth? Who has not
  transgressed?*
*Who is there to follow on Earth knowing the
  Way of the God?*
*I will worship the God of Heaven, but I will
  not tolerate the wickedness
  that reigns in Men on Earth.*
*I will seek out the regions where flows the
  Waters of Life.*
*I wash clean my iniquity before thee,
  which is seen by my God.*
*Forgive me, my Lord, for the sins I have
  committed on Earth,*
*Willingly or unknowingly, from the time of
  my youth until now.*
*Let not me fall into despair, but destroy the
  sin and fault in me,*
*Lighten the labor of my turmoil and illuminate
  my gloom.*
*Let the sins of my father and mother and
  their generations,*
Not fall upon me, may they pass on one side.
*Speak to me now, my Lord! Make me clean
  and pure!*

*Let the merciful hands of my Lord fall grant me
    well-being,
So that I may ever stand strong before thee with
    prayer.
May the good folk spread throughout the world
    bend their knee,
Let them worship thee who may destroy their sin.
MARDUK, Lord of the Magicians and Priests,
    destroy my sin.
ERU(A), Great Goddess of the Earth, destroy
    my sin.
NABU, Fair One, Herald of your Father, MARDUK,
    destroy my sin.
TESHMET, Consort of Nabu, Lady of Borsippa,
    Hear my prayer, destroy my sin.
SARPANIT, Consort of Marduk, Lady of Babylon,
    destroy my sin.
NERGAL-ERRA [The Annihilator], destroy my sin.
You ANUNNAKI [gods] who dwell in the Heavens
    with ANU,
May you come forth and destroy my sin, do away
    with my sin.
May your heart be at peace,
May the heart of my mother and father be
    at peace,
Bring me a life of sinless peace, and then,
Brave MARDUK,
    will I honor thee with submission.*

NABU—is brought before the image of the imprisoned "MARDUK" statue to receive the mysteries from the "unseen god."

THE NINTH, TENTH, ELEVENTH & TWELFTH DAY

A great victory procession of MARDUK and NABU commences on the ninth day, including honorary recitation of the *Enuma Eliš* finale, proclaiming the *"Fifty Names of Marduk"* (Mardukite Tablet-F). Their statues and those of their consorts—SARPANIT and TESHMET—are cleaned on the tenth day before they are to receive a final grand celebratory procession on the eleventh day. Then after the priests conduct closing "consecration" rites at dawn on the twelfth day, all of the images/statues are retired to their appropriate places and Babylonian work-a-day life returns to normal.

Additional Notes:

The Babylonian "Akitu"/"Akiti" Spring Equinox festival replaced national significance of the former Sumerian "Zagmuk" New Year festival and eventually, given the emphasis on Marduk and Mardukite themes, the two rites were symbolically joined together as one. This time marked the beginning of the planting/sowing half of the year—and also the triumph or light over dark, or else order over chaos, represented by the victory of Marduk over Tiamat (and also the ability of Inanna-Ishtar to descend to the Otherworld/Underworld and return, further emphasizing the resurrection themes of the season and origins for the modern "Easter" observations—carrying a pagan name "Ostara" that is named for Ishtar). As a national 12-day ceremonial observation, the Akiti/Akitu public festival rituals occupied a significant portion of the religious year, combining the modern equivalence of Christmas and Easter into one grand holiday observation.

*Here are recorded the
Tablets of Creation as given
by the Priests of Nabu,
which describes the victory
of Marduk over Tiamat.*

THE BOOK OF

ENUMA ELIŠ

(TABLET-N)

ENUMA ELIŠ SERIES – TABLET I

When in the heights the Heavens had not been named,
And the Earth had not yet been named, And the primeval
APSU, who birthed them, And CHAOS, TIAMAT,
The Ancient One, Mother to them all.
Their waters were as One and no field was formed,
No marsh was to be seen;
When of the gods none had been called into being,
And none bore a name, and no destinies were ordained;
Then were created the celestial gods in the midst of
    heaven,
LAHMU and LAHAMU were called into being
And the Ages increased.
Then ANSAR and KISAR were created,
And the god ANU then came forth who begat NUDIMMUD
    [ENKI].
Abounding in all wisdom he had no rival.
Thus the Great Gods were established.
But TIAMAT and APSU were still in confusion,
Troubled and in disorder.
APSU was not diminished in might, and TIAMAT roared.
APSU, the begetter of the great gods,
Cried unto MUMMU, his minister,
And said: "MUMMU, thou minister that causes my spirit
    to rejoice,
Come with me to TIAMAT."
So they went and consulted on a plan with regard to the
    gods, their sons.
APSU spoke: "Let me destroy their ways, let there be
    lamentation,
And then let us lie down again in peace."
When TIAMAT heard these words, she raged and cried
    aloud.
She uttered a curse and unto APSU she asked:
"What then shall we do?"
MUMMU answered giving counsel unto APSU,

"Come, their way is strong, but you can destroy it;
This day you shall have rest, by night shalt thou lie down
    in peace."
They banded themselves together
And at the side of TIAMAT they advanced; they were
    furious;
They devised mischief without resting night and day.
They prepared for battle, fuming and raging;
They joined their forces and made weapons invincible;
She spawned monster-serpents, sharp of tooth, and
    merciless of fang;
With poison, instead of blood, she filled their bodies.
Fierce monster-vipers she clothed with terror.
With splendor she clothed them, she made them of lofty
    stature.
Whoever beheld them, terror overcame him,
Their bodies reared up and none could withstand their
    attack.
She set up vipers and dragons, and the monster
    LAHAMU.
And hurricanes, and raging hounds, and scorpion-men,
And mighty tempests, and fish-men, and rams;
They bore cruel weapons, without fear of the fight.
Her commands were mighty, none could resist them;
After this fashion she made eleven kinds of monsters.
Among the gods who were her sons,
Inasmuch as he had given her support,
She exalted KINGU; in their midst she raised him
    to power.
To march before the forces, to lead the host,
To give the battle-signal, to advance to the attack,
To direct the battle, to control the fight,
Unto him she entrusted, saying: "I have uttered thy spell,
In the assembly of the gods I have raised thee to power.
The dominion over all the gods have I entrusted
    unto him.
Be thou exalted, you are my chosen spouse,

May your name be magnified among all ANUNNAKI."
She gave him the Tablets of Destiny, on his breast she
  laid them,
Saying: "Thy command shall not be in vain,
And your decrees shall be established."
Now KINGU, thus exalted, having received the power
  of ANU,
Decreed the fate among the gods his sons,
Saying: "Let the opening of your mouth quench the
  Fire-god;
He who is exalted in the battle, let him display his
  might!"

ENUMA ELIŠ SERIES – TABLET II

TIAMAT made weighty her handiwork,
Evil she wrought against the gods her children.
To avenge APSU, TIAMAT planned evil,
But how she had collected her forces, the god unto EA
  [ENKI] divulged.
ENKI was grievously afflicted and he sat in sorrow.
The days went by, and his anger was appeased,
And to the place of ANSAR his father he took his way.
He went and, standing before ANSAR, his father,
All that TIAMAT had plotted he repeated unto him,
Saying "TIAMAT, our mother hath conceived a hatred
  for us,
With all her force she rages, full of wrath.
All the gods have turned to her,
With those, whom you created, they go to her side.
They have banded together and at the side of TIAMAT
And they advance; they are furious,
They devise mischief without resting night and day.
They prepare for battle, fuming and raging;
They have joined their forces and are making war.
TIAMAT, who formed all things,

And made weapons invincible;
She hath spawned monster-serpents,
Sharp of tooth, and merciless of fang.
With poison, instead of blood, she hath filled their
  bodies.
Fierce monster-vipers she hath clothed with terror,
With splendor she has armed them;
She has made them tall in stature.
Whoever beholds them is overcome by terror,
Their bodies rear up and none can withstand their
  attack.
She hath set up vipers, and dragons, and the monster
  LAHAMU,
And hurricanes and raging hounds, and scorpion-men,
And mighty tempests, and fish-men and rams;
They bear cruel weapons, without fear of the fight.
Her commands are mighty; none can resist them;
After this fashion, huge of stature,
She has made eleven kinds of monsters.
Among the gods who are her sons,
Inasmuch as he has given her support,
She has exalted KINGU;
In their midst she hath raised him to power.
To march before the forces, to lead the host,
To give the battle-signal, to advance to the attack.
To direct the battle, to control the fight,
To him she has uttered your spell;
She hath given to him the Tablets of Destiny,
On his breast she laid hem,
Saying: 'Thy command shall not be in vain,
And the your word shall be established.'
"O my father, let not the word of thy lips be overcome,
Let me go, that I may accomplish all that is in
  thy heart.
I shall avenge."

ENUMA ELIŠ SERIES – TABLET III

ANSAR spoke to his minister:
"O GAGA, thou minister who causes my spirit to rejoice,
Unto LAHMU and LAHAMU I will send thee.
Make ready for a feast, at a banquet let them sit,
Let them eat bread, let them mix wine,
That for MARDUK, the avenger, they may decree the fate.
Go, GAGA, stand before them, And all that I tell thee,
Repeat unto them, and say: 'ANSAR, your son, has
    sent me,
The purpose of his heart he has made known unto me.
He said that TIAMAT, our mother, has conceived a hatred
    for us,
With all her force she rages full of wrath.
All the gods have turned to her, with those, whom you
    created,
They go to her side. I sent ANU, but he could not
    withstand her;
NUDIMMUD [ENKI] was afraid and turned back.
But MARDUK has set out, the champion of the gods,
    your son;
To set out against TIAMAT his heart has called him.
He opened his mouth and spake unto me,
Saying: 'If I, your avenger, Conquer TIAMAT and give
    you life,
Appoint an assembly, make my fate preeminent and
    proclaim it so.
In UPSUKKINAKU seat yourself joyfully together;
With my word in place I will decree fate.
May whatsoever I do remain unaltered,
May the word of my lips never be changed nor made of
    no avail.'
Quickly decree for him the fate which you bestow
So that he may go and fight your strong enemy."
GAGA went humbly before LAHMU and LAHAMU,
    the gods,

His fathers, and he kissed the ground at their feet.
He humbled himself; then he stood up and spake unto
    them saying:
"ANSAR, your son, has sent me,
The purpose of his heart he hath made known unto me.
He says that TIAMAT, our mother, hath conceived a
    hatred for us,
With all her force she rages full of wrath."
And he spoke the words of the tale.
LAHMU and LAHAMU heard and cried aloud.
All of the IGIGI wailed bitterly, saying:
"We do not understand the deed of TIAMAT!"
Then did they collect and go,
The great gods, all of them, the ANUNNAKI who
    decree fate.
They entered in the House of ANSAR, kissed one another,
They made ready for the feast, ate bread,
And they mixed sesame-wine.
They were wholly at ease, their spirit was exalted;
Then for MARDUK, their avenger, they decreed the fate.

ENUMA ELIŠ SERIES – TABLET IV

The ANUNNAKI prepared for MARDUK a lordly chamber,
Before his fathers as prince he took his place.
"MARDUK, You are now chief among the great gods,
Thy fate is unequaled, thy word is ANU.
Your words shall be command,
In your power shall it be to exalt and to abase.
None among the gods shall transgress your boundary.
Abundance, shall exist in thy sanctuary shrine,
Even if you lack offerings.
MARDUK, you are our avenger!
We give you sovereignty over the whole world.
Sit down in might; be exalted in thy command.
Your weapon shall never lose its power; it shall crush
    your enemy.

Lord, spare the life of him that puts his trust in thee,
But as for the god who began the rebellion, empty them
 of life."
The ANUNNAKI set out a garment
And continued to speak to MARDUK.
"May thy fate, O lord, be supreme among the gods,
To destroy and to create; speak only the word,
And your command shall be fulfilled.
Command now that the garment vanish;
And speak the word again and let the garment reappear!"
Then he spake the words and the garment vanished;
Again he commanded it and the garment reappeared.
When the gods, his fathers, beheld the fulfillment of
 his word,
They rejoiced, and they did homage unto him,
Saying, "Maerdechai! Maerdechai! MARDUK is king!"
They bestowed upon him the scepter, the throne and
 the ring,
They give him invincible weaponry to overwhelm the
 enemy.
"Go, and cut off the life of TIAMAT," they said.
"And let the wind carry her blood into secret places."
MARDUK made ready the bow, his first choice in weapon,
He slung a spear upon him. He raised the club in his
 right hand.
The bow and the quiver he hung at his side.
He set the FLAMING DISC in front of him
And with the flame he filled his body.
He fashioned a net to enclose the inward parts of
 TIAMAT,
He stationed the four winds so that nothing of her
 might escape;
The South wind and the North wind and the East wind
And the West wind He created the evil wind,
And the tempest, and the hurricane,
And the fourfold wind,
And the sevenfold wind, and the cyclone,

And the wind which had no equal;

He sent forth the winds which he had created, seven
in total;

To disturb the inward parts of TIAMAT.

Then MARDUK raised the thunderbolt, mounted the
chariot,

A storm unequaled for terror, and he harnessed four
horses

Named DESTRUCTION, FEROCITY, TERROR,

And SWIFTNESS; and foam came from their mouths

And they were mighty in battle,

Trained to trample underfoot.

With garments cloaked in terror and an overpowering
brightness

Crowning his head, MARDUK set out toward the raging
TIAMAT.

Then the gods beheld him.

And when the lord drew near,

He gazed upon the inward parts of TIAMAT,

He heard the muttering of KINGU, her spouse.

As MARDUK gazed, KINGU was troubled,

The will of KINGU was destroyed and his motions ceased.

And the gods, his helpers, who marched by his side,

Beheld their leader's fear and their sight was troubled.

But TIAMAT did not turn her neck.

She spit rebellious words.

MARDUK raised the thunderbolt,

His mighty weapon, against TIAMAT,

Who was raging, and he called out:

"You have become great as you have exalted yourself
on high,

And your heart has prompted you to call to battle.

You have raised KINGU to be your spouse,

You have chosen Evil and sinned against ANU and
his decree.

And against the gods, my fathers,

You have dedicated yourself to a wicked plan.

Let us face off now then in battle!"
When TIAMAT heard these words,
She acted possessed and lost her sense of reason.
She screamed wild, piercing cries,
She trembled and shook to her very foundations.
She recited an incantation, and cast a spell,
And the gods of the battle cried out for their weapons.
Then TIAMAT and MARDUK advanced towards one
    another,
The battle drew near.
Lord MARDUK spread out his net and caught her,
And the evil wind that gathered behind him he let loose
    in her
Face when she opened her mouth fully.
The terrible winds filled her belly,
And her courage was taken from her,
And her mouth opened wider.
MARDUK seized the spear and burst her belly,
Severing her inward parts, he pierced her heart.
He overcame her and cut off her life;
He cast down her body and stood upon it.
After slaying TIAMAT, the leader of the ANCIENT ONES,
The might was broken and her minions scattered.
But they were surrounded, so that they could not escape.
MARDUK took them captive and broke their weapons;
In the net they were caught and in the snare they
    sat down.
And on the eleven monsters which she had filled
With the power of striking terror, he brought them
    affliction,
Their strength he stole and their opposition
He trampled under his feet.
From KINGU who he had conquered,
He rightly took the Tablets of Destiny
And sealed them with his seal, then hung them from
    his neck.

Now after MARDUK had conquered and cast down his
  enemies,
And had fully established ANSAR's triumph over the
  enemy,
And had attained the purpose of NUDUMMID [EA (ENKI)],
Over the captive gods he strengthened his position,
And he returned to the conquered TIAMAT.
With his merciless club he smashed her skull.
He cut through the channels of her blood,
And he made the North wind steal it away
Outside in secret places between spaces.
His fathers beheld, and rejoiced and were glad;
Presents and gifts they brought unto him.
Then Lord MARDUK rested, gazing upon her dead body
And devised a cunning plan.
He split her up like a flat fish into two halves;
One half of her he established a covering for heaven.
Sealed with a GATE he stationed a WATCHER IAK SAKKAK
And fixed him not to let her waters to ever come forth.
MARDUK passed through and surveyed the regions
  of Heaven,
And over the Deep he set the dwelling of NUDIMMUD
  [ENKI].
And after measuring the structure of the Deep,
He founded his Mansion,
Which was created likened to Heaven and he set down
The fixed districts for ANU, ENLIL and ENKI to reign.

ENUMA ELIŠ SERIES – TABLET V

MARDUK fixed the Star Gates of the Elder Gods;
And the stars he gave images as the stars of the Zodiac,
which he fixed in place.
He ordained the year and into sections he divided it;
For the twelve months he fixed the stars.
He founded his Star Gate on NIBIRU to fix them in zones;
That none might rebel or go astray,

He fixed the Star Gate of ENLIL
And IA [E.A.-ENKI] alongside him.
He opened great gates on both sides,
He made strong gates on the left and on the right
And in the midst thereof he fixed the zenith;
He fixed the Star Gate for the Moon-god
And decreed that he shine forth,
Trusting him with the night and to determine days;
The first of the great gates he assigned to NANNA [SIN]
And every month without ceasing he would be crowned,
   Saying:
"At the beginning of the month, when you shine down
   upon the land,
You command the trumpets of the six days of the moon,
And on the seventh day you will divide the crown.
On the fourteenth day you will stand opposite as
   half-moon.
When the Sun-god of the foundation of heaven calls thee,
On that the final day again you will stand as opposite.
All shall go about the course I fix.
You will drawn near to judge the righteous
And destroy the unrighteous.
That is my decree and the covenant of the first gate."
The gods, his fathers, beheld the net which MARDUK
   had fashioned,
They beheld his bow and how its work was accomplished.
They praised the work which he had done and then ANU
   raised up
And kissed the bow before the assembly of the gods.
And thus he named the names of the bow, saying:
"Long-wood shall be one name,
And the second name shall be Dragonslayer,
And its third name shall be the Bow-star,
In heaven shall it remain as a sign to all."
Then ANU and MARDUK fixed a Star Gate for it too,
And after the ANUNNAKI decreed the fates for the
   ANCIENT ONES,

MARDUK set a throne in heaven for himself at ANU's
right hand.

ENUMA ELIŠ SERIES – TABLET VI

The ANUNNAKI acclaimed him "First among the ELDER
GODS."
MARDUK heard the praises of the gods,
His heart called to him to devised a cunning plan.
He approached IA [ENKI] saying:
"The Key to the GATE shall be ever hidden, except to my
offspring.
I will take my blood and with bone I will fashion a Race
of Men,
That they may keep watch over the GATE.
And from the blood of KINGU I will create a race of men,
That they will inhabit the Earth in service to the gods
So that our shrines may be built and the temples filled.
But I will alter the ways of the gods, and I will change
their paths;
Together shall they be oppressed
And unto evil shall they no longer reign.
I will bind the ELDER GODS to the WATCHTOWERS,
Let them keep watch over the GATE of ABSU,
And the GATE of TI.AM.TU and the GATE of KINGU.
I bind the WATCHER IAK SAKKAK to the GATE
With the Key known only to my Race.
Let none enter that GATE
Since to invoke DEATH is to utter the final prayer."
The ANUNNAKI rejoiced and set their mansions in
UPSUKKINAKU.
When all this had been done, the Elders of the ANUNNAKI
Seated themselves around MARDUK
And in their assembly they exalted him
And named him FIFTY times,
Bestowing upon him the FIFTY powers of the gods.

*Here are recorded
the Fifty Names of Marduk
concluding the epic
Tablets of Creation series of
the Priests of Nabu.*

THE BOOK OF FIFTY NAMES

NINNU

(TABLET-F)

ENUMA ELIŠ SERIES – TABLET VI

1. The First Name is MARDUK-DUGGA-ANU,
   Son of the Sun, Lord of Lords, Master of Magicians,
   Most Radiant Among the Gods is he.
2. The Second Name is MARDUKKA,
   ANUNNAKI Creator,
   Knower of the Secrets of MARDUK,
   Time, Space & Creation [Geometry of the Universe].
3. The Third Name is ARRA-MARUTUKKU,
   Master of Protections and of the Gate to the
   ANCIENT ONES
   And to whom the people give praise as Protector of
   the City.
   Possesses the ARRA-Star.
4. The Fourth Name is BARASHAKUSHU-BAALDURU,
   Worker of Miracles, with wide heart and strong
   sympathies.
5. The Fifth Name is LUGGAL-DIMMERANKI(A)-BANU
   TUKKU,
   Commander of the Wind Demons,
   The Metatronic Voice Heard Among the Gods.
6. The Sixth Name is NARI-LUGGAL-DIMMERANKI(A)-
   BAN-RABISHU,
   Watcher of the Star Gates of the IGIGI & ANUNNAKI,
   And who is named the Monitor of the Gods in their
   stations.
   Keeper of the Gates between worlds.
7. The Seventh Name is ASARU-LUDU-BAN-MASKIM,
   Wielder of the Flaming Sword, The Light of the
   Gods.
   Called for the safety and protection of the
   Gatekeeper.
8. The Eighth Name is NAMTI-LAKU-BAN-UTUK-
   UKUT-UKKU,
   Master of the Death Gate and of Necromancy,

And who is able to revive the Gods with a single prayer.

9. The Ninth Name is NAMRU-BAKA-KALAMU,
The Shining One who is Counselor of the Sciences.
Called to increase the scientific knowledge of the Gatekeeper.

10. The Tenth Name is ASARU-BAALPRIKU,
Creator of grains and plants, who knows no wasteland.
Called to increase the vegetative and blooming growth.

11. The Eleventh Name is ASARU-ALIM-BAR-MARATU,
Who is revered for wisdom in the house of counsel,
And who is looked to for peace when the Gods are unsettled.
Called to aid in communication with the ANUNNAKI and to dispel deception.

12. The Twelfth Name is ASARU-ALIM-NUNA-BANA-TATU,
The Mighty One who is the Light of the Father of the Gods,
And who directs the decrees of ANU, ENLIL and ENKI/EA.
Called to aid in the enforcement of law on Earth.

13. The Thirteenth Name is (NABU)-TUTU,
He who created them anew, and should their wants be pure, then they are satisfied.
Called to reveal the hidden gnosis within the Gatekeeper.

14. The Fourteenth Name is ZI-UKKINA-GIBIL-ANU,
The life of the Assembly of the Gods
Who established for a bright place for the Gods in the heavens.
Called to reveal the secrets of astrology and the celestial sphere.

15. The Fifteenth Name is ZI-AZAG-ZI-KU-IGIGI-
MAGAN-PA,

Bringer of Purification, God of the Favoring Breeze,

Carrier of Wealth & Abundance to the people.

16. The Sixteenth Name is AGAKU-AZAG-MASH-
GARZANNA,

Lord of the Pure Incantation, The Merciful One,

And whose name is on the mouth of the Created
Race.

Called to bring life to elementaries and ward spirits.

17. The Seventeenth Name is TUKUMU-AZAG-MASH-
SHAMMASHTI,

Knower of the Incantation to destroy all evil ones.

Called in the Maqlu Rite to dispel evil sorceries.

18. The Eighteenth Name is SAHG-ZU-MASH-
SHANANNA,

Founder of the Assembly of Gods and knows their
heart,

And whose name is heralded among the IGIGI.

Called for aiding the Gatekeepers psychic
development.

19. The Nineteenth Name is ZI-SI-MASH-INANNA,

Reconciler of enemies, who puts an end to anger;
Bringer of Peace.

20. The Twentieth Name is SUH-RIM-MASH-SHA-
NERGAL,

Destroyer of wicked foes, who confuses their plans.

May be sent to destroy the enemies of the
Gatekeeper.

21. The Twenty-first Name is SUH-KUR-RIM-MASH-
SHADAR,

Who confounds the wicked foes in their places.

May be sent to destroy the unknown enemies of the
Gatekeeper.

22. The Twenty-second Name is ZAH-RIM-MASH-
SHAG-ARANNU,

Lord of Lightning, A warrior among warriors.
May be raised against entire armies of men.

23. The Twenty-third Name is ZAH-KUR-RIM-MASH-
TI-SHADDU,

Destroyer of the Enemy in battle,
Who slays in a most unnatural fashion.

24. The Twenty-fourth Name is ENBILULU-MASH-
SHA-NEBU,

Knower of the secrets of water and of secret places
for grazing.

Called to bestow the secrets of dowsing and aid
irrigation.

25. The Twenty-fifth Name is EPADUN-E-YUNGINA-
KANPA,

Lord of Irrigation, who sprinkles water in the
heavens and on Earth.

As the previous, also the secrets of Sacred Geometry.

26. The Twenty-sixth Name is ENBI-LULU-GUGAL-
AGGA,

Lord of growth and cultivation, who raises the
grains to maturity,

And some have said is a face of ENKI.

27. The Twenty-seventh Name is HEGAL-BURDISHU,

Master of farming and the plentiful harvest
And who provides for the people's consumption.
May also be called to aid in personal fertility.

28. The Twenty-eighth Name is SIRSIR-APIRI-KUBAB-
ADAZU-ZU-KANPA,

The domination of TIAMAT by the power of the Net.
Called for mastery of the Serpent and the Kundalini.

29. The Twenty-ninth Name is MAL-AHK-BACH-
ACHA-DUGGA,

Lord of bravery and courage, Rider of the Ancient
Worm.

Summoned for courage, bravery and self-confidence.

30. The Thirtieth Name is GIL-AGGA-BAAL,
Furnisher of the life-giving seed, Beloved
(betrothed) consort to INANNA-ISHTAR.
Called for women who desire pregnancy.

31. The Thirty-first Name is GILMA-AKKA-BAAL,
Mighty One and Divine Architect of the temples.
Possesses secrets concerning the Geometry of the
Universe.

32. The Thirty-second Name is AGILMA-MASH-SHAY
-E-GURRA,
Maker of Rain Clouds to nourish the fields of the
Earth.
Called forth in times of drought.

33. The Thirty-third Name is ZULUM-MU-ABBA-BAAL,
Giver of excellent counsel and power in all
businesses,
And Destroyer of the wicked foe, maintaining
goodness and order.

34. The Thirty-fourth Name is MUMMU,
Creator of the Universe from the flesh of TI.AM.TU.
Keeper of the Four Watchtower Gates to the Outside.

35. The Thirty-fifth Name is ZU-MUL-IL-MAR-AN-
DARA-BAAL,
The heavens have none equal in strength and
vitality.
Called forth to aid in healing rituals and rites.

36. The Thirty-sixth Name is AGISKUL-AGNI-BAAL-
LUGAL-ABDUBAR,
Who sealed the ANCIENT ONES in the abyss.
Called by the piously righteous for strength and
vigor.

37. The Thirty-seventh Name is PAGALGUENNA-AR
RA-BA-BAAL,

Possessor of Infinite Intelligence, preeminent among
the Gods.

Offers wisdom in oracles and divination.

38. The Thirty-eighth Name is LUGAL-DURMAH-
ARATA-AGAR-BAAL,

King of the gods, Lord of Rulers [Durmah].

Aids the Gatekeeper in developing all mystic powers.

39. The Thirty-ninth Name is ARRA-ADU-NUNA-
ARAMAN-GI,

Counselor of ENKI/EA, who created the Gods, his
fathers,

And whose princely ways no other God can equal.

Called during (self)-initiations to aid you through
the Gates.

40. The Fortieth Name is DUL-AZAG-DUMU-DUKU-
ARATA-GIGI,

Possessor the secret knowledge and the wand of
Lapis Lazuli.

Can reveal untold marvels of the cosmos to the
Gatekeeper.

41. The Forty-first Name is LUGAL-ABBA-BAAL-DIKU,

Eldest of the Elder Ones, and pure is his dwelling
among them.

Aids the Gatekeeper in acquiring "self-honesty."

42. The Forty-second Name is LUGALDUL-AZAGA-
ZI-KUR,

Knower of the secrets of the spirits of wind and star.

Offers the Gatekeeper secrets to command spirits.

43. The Forty-third Name is IR-KINGU-BAR-E-RIMU,

Holding the capture of KINGU, supreme is his might.

Keeper of the Blood(Birth)-Rights.

44. The Forty-fourth Name is KI-EN-MA-EN-GAIGAI,

Supreme Judge of the ANUNNAKI, at whose name
the gods quake.

To be called when no other spirit will arrive.

45. The Forty-fifth Name is E-ZIS-KUR-NENIGEGAI,
Knows the lifespan of all things,
And who fixed the Created Race's life at 120 years.

46. The Forty-sixth Name is GIBIL-GIRRA-BAAL-
AGNI-TARRA,
Lord of the sacred fire and the forge, creator of the
Sword.
Also possesses the secrets of the "fiery passions."

47. The Forty-seventh Name is ADDU-KAKO-DAMMU,
Raiser of storms that blanket the skies of Heaven.

48. The Forty-eighth Name is ASH-ARRU-BAX-
TAN-DABAL,
Keeper of time, the secrets of the past and future.
May be summoned to aid acts of divination.

49. The Forty-ninth Name is The STAR, let NEBIRU be
his name,
He who forced his way through the midst of
TIAMAT,
May he hold the ALPHA and the OMEGA in his hands.
Summoned to discern the Destiny of the Universe.

50. The Fiftieth Name is FIFTY and NINNU-AM-
GASHDIG,
The Judge of Judges, Determiner of the laws of the
Realm.
The Patron of the Dragonblood Kings of Earth.

APOCRYPHA OF THE MARDUK TABLET

The Forty-ninth Name is the STAR, that which shines
   in the heavens.
May he hold the ALPHA and the OMEGA in his hands,
And may all pay homage unto him, saying:
"He who forced his way through the midst of TI.AM.TU
   without resting,
Let NIBIRU be his name – The Seizer of the Crossings
That causes the stars of heaven to uphold their paths.
He comes as a shepherd to the gods who are like sheep.
In the future of mankind at the End of Days,
May this be heard without ceasing; may it hold sway
   forever!
Since MARDUK created the realm of heaven and
   fashioned the firm earth,
He is forever the Lord of this World."
ENLIL listened. ENKI heard and rejoiced.
All of the Spirits of Heaven waited.
ENLIL gave to MARDUK his name and title BEL.
ENKI gave to MARDUK his name and title EA and
Said: "The binding of all my decrees, let MARDUK now
   control.
All of my commands, shall he make known."
The Fiftieth Name is FIFTY and NINNU-AM-GASHDIG,
The Judger of Judges, Determiner of the laws of the
   Realm.
By the name FIFTY did the ANUNNAKI then proclaim
   MARDUK's "Fifty Names."
The ANUNNAKI made his path preeminent.
Let the Fifty Names of MARDUK be held in
   remembrance to all
And let the leaders proclaim them;
Let the wise gather to consider them together,

Let the father repeat them and teach them to his son;
Let them be in the ears of the priest and the shepherd.
Let all men rejoice in MARDUK, the Lord of the gods,
That be may cause the land, his Earth, to be
    prosperous,
And that he himself may enjoy prosperity!
His word hold and his command is unaltered;
No utterance from his mouth goes unnoticed.
His gaze is of anger and turns his back to none;
No god can withstand his wrath.
And yet, wide is his heart and broad is his compassion;
The sinner and evil-doer in his presence weep for
    themselves.

THE BOOK OF

GATES

(LIBER L/G)

*Here are recorded the
Teachings of Marduk as given
to his firstborn heir Nabu,
Keeper of the Secrets of Writing
and the Wisdom of Eridu
used to raise Marduk in Babylon
and to guide the Priests.*

THE BOOK OF

NABU-TUTU

(TABLET-T)

NABU-TUTU SERIES – TABLET I

And so NABU {indicated as I} went to the Mountain
  [pyramid],
To hear the Voice of the Great God come from the
  Mountain.
The Unseen God, whose vision and voice comes to the
  prophet.
And the voice of MARDUK came out of the Mountain
  [pyramid].
"I am the voice of the God who cannot be here.
I am the voice of the God who is in the hearts of all men.
I am the voice of the God who appears in many faces.
It is I, the voice of the God, that will teach you the way,
And I command you, dear son, to write this what I say
On tablets for all of humanity's sake,
That they might honor the Gods of their Ancestors
  [ANUNNAKI]
But worship the Eternal Source of All Being & Creation.
I am not only the voice of your God, but also your
  commander.
Prepare for the long and hard battle such as lies ahead."
NABU asked MARDUK:
"What can men do to prepare for the sake of their
  own lives,
How can they live to serve and worship proper?"
And the voice of MARDUK echoed out:
"Live piously and by the Union Code [Tablet] of the
  ANUNNAKI.
For there is no longer any religion higher than the
  Source.
And the desire of God is for us to love one another,
And not to sacrifice the life which has been made
  possible.
A certain knowledge of what is good and evil on Earth,
With perfected choice will be the former, so is the will
  of God.

There is no pleasure to be gained from the wasteful shed
   of blood.
Celebrate life and sing praises to the creation around
   you,
Which has been carefully made for you, by the Highest,
Under who the ANUNNAKI live and reign over the
   Lower."
And NABU asked MARDUK:
"For what can men do to repent of their sins if not by
   sacrifice?"
The voice of MARDUK responded:
"Give to the Eternal Source dedication and commitment
   in life,
And this is all that is asked of you in this life.
Men approach the face of God in fear and beg
   forgiveness,
When their efforts could be better spent in prayer and
   praise.
Men flood the temple-shrines with more food than is
   consumed,
When it could be better distributed among the poor.
[something later instilled by Babylonian kings...]
Bring the God of Life no more vain offerings of flesh.
Pray and live a pious life at one with creation. How hard
   is this?
Make simple rituals if it pleases you,
For only prayer and devotion is asked of the God of All.
Do not deny yourself of a happy existence in the name
   of God.
Never let your livelihood be neglected because you
   worship God.
Lives dedicated to the Source are not preoccupied by
   worship,
For to go out and live and act the pious life among men
   is best."

NABU-TUTU SERIES – TABLET II

All things that are, are moved; Only that which is not, is
  unmovable.
Every Body is changeable.
Not every Body is able to be dissolved into elements.
Some Bodies are able to be dissolved into elements.
Every living thing is not mortal.
Not every living thing is immortal.
That which may be dissolved is also corruptible.
That which is Eternal is unchangeable, incorruptible.
That which is unchangeable is eternal.
That which is always physical is always corrupted.
That which is made but once,
Is never corrupted and does not become any other thing.
First, God; Second, the World; Third, Man.
The World for Man, Man for God.
Of the Soul-Program,
That part has been given as the conscience of mortals,
But that which is Reasonable is immortal.
Every essence is immortal.
Every essence is unchangeable.
Every thing that is, is double.
None of the things that are stand still.
Not all things are moved by a Soul-Program,
But everything that is, is controlled by its own Soul-
  Program.
Every thing that suffers is Sensible,
Every thing that is Sensible suffers.
Every thing that is sad is also able to rejoice,
And must be a mortal living Creature.
Not every thing that is able to be joyous can also be sad,
Like unto the eternal living things.
Not every Body can be sick;
but every sick Body is dissoluble.
The Mind resides in the All [God].
Reasoning in experience is in Man,

Experience becomes the Reason in the Mind.

The Mind is void of suffering.

No thing in a Body is true.

All that is incorporeal, is void of Lying.

Every thing that is made is corruptible.

Nothing good made upon Earth, nothing evil made in Heaven.

God is good, Man is evil.

Good is voluntary, or of its own accord.

Evil is involuntary or against its will.

The Gods choose good things, as good things.

Time is a Divine thing.

Law is Human.

Malice is the nourishment of the Material Kingdom .

Time is the Corruption of Man.

Whatsoever is in Heaven is unalterable.

All upon Earth is alterable.

Nothing in Heaven is for a charge, nothing on Earth is free.

Nothing unknown in Heaven, nothing known upon Earth.

The things upon Earth communicate not with those in Heaven.

All things in Heaven are without blame,

All things upon Earth are subject to consequence.

That which is immortal, is not mortal:

That which is mortal is not immortal.

That which is sown, is not always brought to fruition;

But that which is manifest had always been sown.

Of the perishable Body, there are two Times,

One from sowing to generation, one from generation to death.

Of an everlasting Body, the time is only from the Generation.

Perishable Bodies are increased and diminished,

Perishable matter is divided into contraries;

As in Corruption and Generation, but Eternal matter exists unto its self.

NABU-TUTU SERIES – TABLET III

The Generation of Man is Corruption,
The Corruption of Man is the beginning of Generation.
That which off-springs or produces another,
Is itself an product of another.
Of things that are, some are in Bodies, some in their
Ideas.
Whatsoever things belong to operation or working, are in
a Body.
That which is immortal, partakes not of that which is
mortal.
That which is mortal, does not come into an immortal
Body,
But that which is immortal can come into a mortal Body.
Operations or Workings are not carried upwards,
But descend downwards.
Things upon Earth do nothing to advantage those in
Heaven,
But all things in Heaven can do profit
And advantage for the things upon Earth.
Heaven is capable and a fit receptacle of everlasting
Bodies,
The Earth is one of corruptible Bodies.
The Earth is brutish, the Heaven is rational.
Those things that are in Heaven are subjected or placed
under it,
But the things on Earth, are placed over it's matrix
Heaven is the first Element.
Providence is Divine Order.
Necessity is the Minister or Servant of Providence.
Fortune is the vehicle or consequence of what is without
Order;
The focus of operation,
Nothing more than opinionated glamour or a fantasy.
Avoid all conversation, both idle and wise,
With the multitudes or common people of the masses,

For that which is Above
Would not have you become either the subject of Envy,
Much less to be considered ridiculous by the many.
The like have always been pulled toward themselves,
That which is like,
Such as when the waters settle upon their levels.
The unlike will never agree with the unlike natures,
Such is the pattern of their way:
Such as you will find
With the variegated philosophical discourses.
And dogmatic treatise that circulate among the masses.
The unlike natures are unique in one facet:
That they act as a sharpening stone for the evil
    tendencies in men,
Another vehicle for their maliciousness.
Conclusively it is better to avoid the multitudes
And realize that they are not in the path of
    understanding the virtue
And power of the things that have been said here.
And concerning the nature
And composition of those living things called "humans,"
It may be simply said that they are prone to
    maliciousness,
being something they are both familiar with and
    nourished by.
When first the world was made,
All things were in perfected accordance
With Providence and Necessity, Destiny [or Fate],
Bearing Rule over all. Knowing this perfection,
The mortal creatures will be the worse for it,
Despising the whole because it was made.
And if the only power known to them is to be the evil
    cause
Of disorder upon Fate or Destiny,
Than they will never abstain from the tendencies
Toward evil doings.

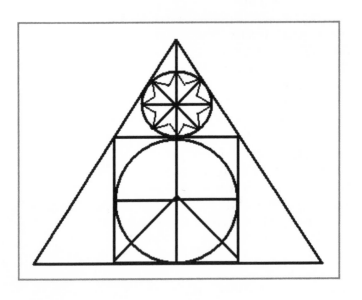

THE BOOK OF

CROSSINGS

(TABLET-X)

Our physical universe operates on fundamental geometry of metaphysical vibration. Defined natures of energetic currents (vibrations) are what wizards and mystics understand as magical correspondences. Energetic polarity of a specific current is allocated across many systems of correspondence, for example: colors, planets, days of the week. Emphasis should not be on the fragmentation of "levels." The separation of the whole into parts only to find more separate relationships and correspondences is not the best way back to true unification.

Accessing powers of the Gates requires activation and/or dissolution (depending on semantic preference) of the astral form or Body of Light as the "I AM" paradigm and then envisioning the Gate in the astral world. Increased familiarity, true knowledge and experience developed from working with individual currents—and the lore they represent—increases the Gatekeepers chances for energetic conscious connection/communication. The Seeker approaches each "Veil of Existence" on their ascent back to the Source.

Preparation of a proper portal (or mental impression on the subconscious) may include any number of the glyphs from the BABILI tablets (given throughout the current volume). True-knowledge of the system and self-honesty are adamantly necessary for perceiving existence as it truly is, from the perspective of its designers, as opposed to the way in which a player is programmed to experience it.

Rituals, energy work and meditation may incorporate any key glyphs, symbols, and incantations, for each individual "step" on the "Ladder of Lights" or "Star-Tower." Supplemental Mardukite material may also aid the modern Gatekeeper in "tuning in" to the frequency-vibration of each Gate current successfully.

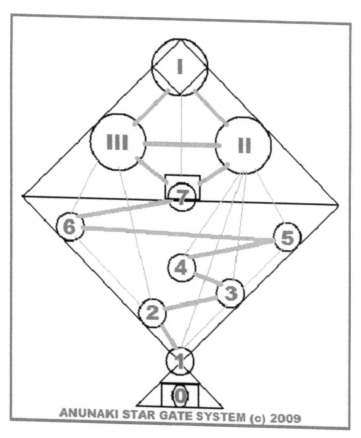

ANUNAKI STAR GATE SYSTEM (c) 2009

Descriptions of the original Mesopotamian "Ladder of Lights" model are seldom explored in contemporary mysticism. In the Star-Gate depiction shown here, the Gatekeeper will see a dual pyramid, one in the "heights" of Heaven, and one in the "depths" of material existence [Earth]—but these are actually one and the same "pyramid of existence" (not to mention the "spaces between"), encompassed by the etheric ALL that entangles all existence as One—All-as-One. "Heights" (AN) meet "Depths" (KI) and are unified in an all-encompassing existence bound together and interconnected as the ALL.

The many "Gates" can just as easily be seen as "one" or even "none" since it is the fragmented mind which separates our experience from the whole. By "ascending" the course, we are consciously making efforts to "travel backwards" to the Source from which we were removed, or rather which was removed from us via the fragmentation into varied "shells."

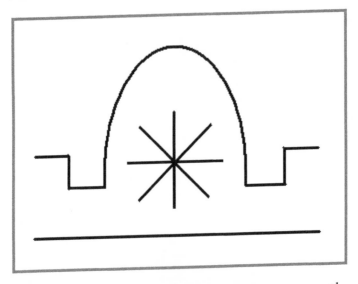

From the "Earthed" point-of-view, we must access the "Ladder of Lights" by ascending the pyramid, essentially backwards, from our side, meaning to first access it through the Earth Gate—the alpha spirit of man or True Self as "I AM"—which is numbered: zero. Also--when magicians call forth powers of the Universe from within a "mandala" or microcosmic ritual "circle," they call upon and open Four Quarters, Quadrangles or Watchtowers. Boundaries of this dimensional universe are bound by the Earth Gate—which is perceived by the Four Directions sealing material existence—and the Self as the Fifth (elemental gate) experiencing the others; and the Gates of the Heights above and the Depths below—All-as-One.

THE NORTH GATE

Gate of the Formless Hunter and of the Abyss,
Thee I invoke the Bornless One
Who brings the "Cleansing Darkness."
Spirits of the Northern Gate, open your mysteries unto me.
Gate of the Scales of Judgment and the Outside,
From which comes the Hosts and Fiends,
Manifest the Shield of ARRA, Truth and Spirit in my hands,
And protect me from the fires of the Destroyer.
Gatekeeper of the Northern Gate, remember:
Open wide the Gate.
Spirit of the Gate of the North, Thou art conjured!

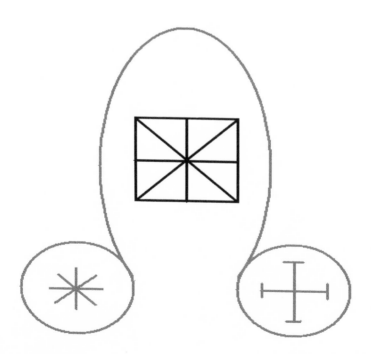

THE EAST GATE

Gate of the Rising Star and of the Rising Sun,
Spirits of the Eastern Gate, Open your mysteries unto me.
Gate of the Forgotten Memory, stir your light in my head,
Kindle the warm fires of remembrance in my being,
Protect me from the "light-so-blinding"
And bring clarity to the washed out childhood memory.
Gatekeeper of the Eastern Gate, remember:
Open wide the Gate.
Spirit of the Gate of the East, Thou are conjured!

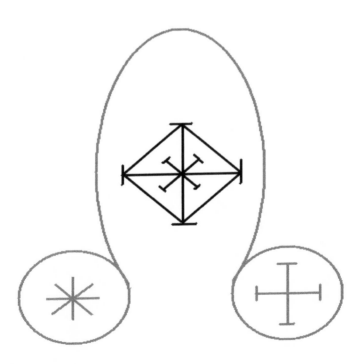

THE SOUTH GATE

Gate of the Fiery Angel and of the StarFire,
Spirits of the Southern Gate, Open your mysteries unto me.
Gate of the Fires of BEL,
Manifest the Sword of Fire, Truth and Spirit in my hands,
And protect me from the Destroyer and the destroyed.
In the names of the most holy armies of
MARDUK and ENKI,
Stand firmly by my side during the Decision [Judgment].
Gatekeeper of the Southern Gate, remember:
Open wide the Gate.
Spirit of the Gate of the South, Thou are conjured!

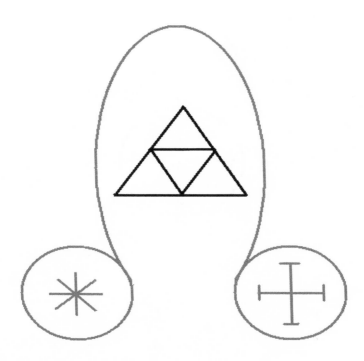

THE WEST GATE

Gate of the Twilight Shadows and of the Setting Sun,
Spirits of the Western Gate, Open your mysteries unto me.
Gate of the Symphony of Light and Darkness,
Kindle the "cold dark blue flame" in my head
And protect me from the sorrow of remembrance.
Gatekeeper of the Western Gate, remember:
Open wide the Gate.
Spirit of the Gate of the West, Thou are conjured!

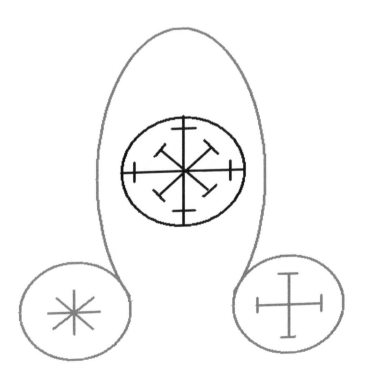

Would you like to know more???

ENTER THE REALM OF THE

**MARDUKITE
CHAMBERLAINS**

NABU—JOSHUA FREE ("Merlyn Stone")
Chief Scribe & Librarian of New Babylon

PUBLISHED BY THE **JOSHUA FREE** IMPRINT REPRESENTING

Mardukite Truth Seeker Press — **mardukite.com**

[Mardukite Liber-W+Z]